PIGS PUBS & TROTTER BUMPS

A PORK CRACKLING
BASED COOKBOOK
(YES, REALLY)

BROUGHT TO YOU BY
THE SNAFFLING PIG
ALONG WITH OUR FRIEND
ELIZABETH FOX

LET'S MAKE THE PIGGIN' MAGIC HAPPEN

WELCOME TO THE HOUSE OF PUN

CONTENTS

ONCE UPON A SWINE

HELLO YOU HERO,

Before we start, let's be honest: this is a frankly ridiculous book. There are a LOT of books out there: ones that offer to change your life, ones that will take you to far-off galaxies and even ones that may cause you to consider turning the spare room into some kind of piggin' sex dungeon. But, there's never been (as far as we can tell) a book about cooking with porky snacks.

Because that would be ridiculous. But hey, it's been a ridiculous few years.

And, we like the ridic. We must do, as otherwise we can't really explain why we sacked off perfectly good 'normal' working lives, to chuck everything into a pork snack-based business when we knew precisely nothing about the industry, or about pubs or about supermarkets or about food supply ... you get the idea. To use geeky online speak, we were total n00bs.

What we did know, though, is that the humble pork crackling and scratching are AWESOME, but that they had been a bit neglected — left in the shadows while newfangled 'cooler' foods had their ten minutes of fame. That belief morphed into an obsession — to the point where we decided we wanted to be the ones to right that wrong. And so, in early 2015, we went for it and set off to show that you can teach an old pig new tricks (and constantly write copy with a lot of ropey pig-based puns and get away with it).

We were full of enthusiasm, but it's fair to say we couldn't have imagined what was to follow. Looking back, much of it blurs into one great big porky rollercoaster, but certain events stand out...

Like the day we spent hours making our initial sample bags only for the first pub we went into to take them all. It was such a mixture of emotions — super exciting, weirdly a tiny bit disappointing and then a touch scary when we realised we needed to go and find the money for a lot more stock. But, most of all, it was bloody good fun, and that's something we've tried to ensure every day since.

Or there's the day we realised (via the medium of a threatening phone call) that we'd trodden on another pig's toes and that our name was going to have to change when we'd just put all our savings into our first foil packaging. OK, that one was probably a bit less fun.

There are the highs — like the thrill of the first time
we walked into a pub we didn't know for a pint and saw
our product nestled on the bar; and there are the lows — like an eight-hour
round trip for a meeting with someone who turns up 30 minutes late
and then tells you they have 15 minutes … in the canteen.

And then, of course, there's the day we trotted into 'Dragons' Den'.

As you might have guessed, it was quite a process to get to that day —
starting with filling out a form online, then telephone interviews, then
a screen test at the BBC (which in our case was in a room wonderfully called
'Alan Partridge') and then weeks of practising with anyone who would
listen. But finally we found ourselves in a cab on the way to the studio,
about to pitch porky wares to multi-millionaires. And we felt ready.

It's worth saying that the Den is 'real'. OK, so the lift isn't an actual lift, it's
just a nice bloke called Dave* opening the doors of a box, and you can't lean
on the walls as they'd fall over, but in terms of the pitch side of things, it
is 100 per cent as you'd hope it is: the Dragons know nothing about who's
about to walk out, we didn't meet anyone beforehand and there's absolutely
no direction or interference from any crew once you start. You press the
lift button, wait for Dave to work his magic and then you're on your own. We
wouldn't have done it if it were anything else, as we weren't there just to
become someone's 15 minutes of Sunday night entertainment; we were 18
months in, had some awesome customers and wanted to talk Pig Business.

Now, if you're reading this, we're guessing there's a fair chance you've seen
what happened (well, the 15-minute edit of the 90 minutes we were in there)
so we'll not bore you with the details, but in short, after a couple of wobbles
we did a deal with the legend that is Nick Jenkins and used more terrible
puns than anybody in the history of TV.

Driving home that night we wanted to tell the world, but we had to wait
three months until our episode came out. And when it did two things
happened: some people on Twitter abused us for how were dressed (it turns
out there are a few people who realllllllly don't like turned up jeans) and
a LOT of people decided they wanted a snaffle.

We've not looked back since.

Going on the Den does not make a business (the phone certainly didn't ring off the hook), but we've lost count of the amount of times it's kicked off a conversation and it confirmed to us what we always hoped was true: a lot of people love a porky snack. And that confirmation gave us confidence to be braver, bolder and, yup, a bit ridiculous.

With that new-found wind in our sails (and sales), we got adventurous: we made whopping great big advent calendars, supplied wedding favours, launched a beer and a hot sauce and even ended up live on QVC a few times with the man himself, Andi Peters; but then we spotted something awesome – some of our snafflers were cooking with crackling as an ingredient, and once we'd seen that happening, the seed of an idea for this very book was well and truly planted.

Working with our supremely talented chef friend Lizzie, we set about figuring out what a pork snack-powered cookbook looks like – we started with the more obvious stuff, but soon Lizzie was whipping up all kinds of inspiration and showing what a versatile swine this old favourite is. You'll see we decided to get some of our amazing pub friends involved too as having a book like this without mentioning pubs would be too ridiculous, even for us.

The combined efforts of this process are a mere couple of page turns away for your snaffling pleasure, with some using crackling as a central ingredient and others having just a little porky injection, but we reckon they all deliver a plate/bowl/handful of swine dining.

And so, with that final (and favourite) pun, this feels like a good place to leave you to it. Thanks so much for playing your part in our adventure; if you see us in the pub we owe you a beer.

Much love
Nick, Andy and Team SP. xx

Dave may not actually have been his name.

PUBS...

Pubs — we are not ashamed to say we love them. We've got more memories than you can shake a piggin' stick at from spending time in them and Snaffling Pig was born in one — it literally was one of those couple of pints down 'why don't we' conversations, except this one, we actually DID. And, it's fair to say that without the incredible support of the wonderful people of pub land we'd not be here today.

So when we decided this (ridiculous) book was going to happen (a conversation that may also have started in the pub), we decided we wanted to get some of our pub customers involved too, so we asked them to flex their culinary muscles.

They did not let us down.

You can find their efforts in the form of five awesome recipes nestled within the next chunk of pages.

SNACKS AND SARNIES

HOME-MADE CRACKLING

WITH ALE AND APPLE DIPPING SAUCE

SERVES 6

HOME-MADE CRACKLING
500g pork rind, unscored
1 tablespoon fine sea salt

ALE AND APPLE SAUCE
225g cooking apples,
   peeled, cored and
   roughly chopped
2–3 teaspoons caster
   sugar, to taste
5 tablespoons ale

We thought it only fitting that we kicked off with a recipe for crackling you can make at home, as it's very hard to beat freshly cooked, still warm porky goodness. Granted, it's a bit of faff to do when you just fancy a quick snaffle (although these will keep for a few days in an airtight container), but hey, that's where we come in.

This is a simple enough oven method and you can order pork rind easily from a local butcher. We primarily use shank rind (from the leg), but different rinds produce different results, so if you like a lighter, fluffier style, go for a leaner cut. Once you've mastered making the base crackling, it's time to bust out the flavours: chilli, paprika and fennel work particularly well and are easy to play with at home. Our own fennel flavoured crackling is awesome and award winning, though if we're honest, it sells pretty terribly as not everyone is sure what it'll be like. Dear friend, consider this your chance to find out!

The quick and nifty apple sauce is the perfect accompaniment to our crackling. It also goes really well in our Pulled Pork Buns too (see page 75).

Remove any excess fat from the pork rind, so it's about 1cm thick. Put the rind into a large colander and pour over a kettleful of boiling water, then pat dry with kitchen paper. Transfer to a baking sheet, rub over ½ tablespoon of the sea salt, and put in the fridge (uncovered) for 1 hour to dry out.

Preheat the oven to 140°C/120°C Fan/Gas Mark 1. Dry the pork rind once again with kitchen paper, then chop into small bite-size pieces. Toss the pork in the remaining salt, then place on a rack set over a large roasting tin and roast for 1 hour.

After the hour, pour out the fat that has drained into the tin. Turn up the heat to 200°C/180°C Fan/Gas Mark 6 and continue to roast the crackling for about 30 minutes until deep golden and crispy. Remove from the oven and allow to cool.

For the apple sauce, put the apples, 2 teaspoons of sugar and 4 tablespoons of the ale in a medium pan over a medium heat. Cover and cook for 10–15 minutes, stirring occasionally, until soft and pulpy. Remove from the heat and stir in the remaining ale and another teaspoon of sugar if needed.

SCOTCH EGGS

MAKES 8

11 eggs
800g sausages
a small bunch of sage,
    roughly chopped
1 tablespoon English mustard
50g plain flour
100g panko breadcrumbs, or use
    regular breadcrumbs if you like
50g Snaffling Pig Ham & Coleman's
    Mustard Crackling
sunflower oil, to fry
salt and pepper, to season

We couldn't not include this pub favourite. Although they are time-consuming to make, they are well worth it, and you can really taste the crackling in the coating!

Place 8 eggs in a medium pan of cold water, and bring to the boil. As soon as the water is boiling, turn down to a simmer for 5 minutes. Remove the eggs and put into a bowl of ice-cold water for 15 minutes.

In a large bowl squeeze the meat from the sausages, mix in 1 beaten egg, the sage, mustard and some seasoning. Divide the meat into 8.

Place the flour in a shallow bowl. Once the eggs are cool, peel and dip each egg into a little flour to coat. Take one of the meatballs and squash in your hand, place an egg into the centre of the meat and use your hands to ease the meat around the egg (making sure there is an even coating of meat around the egg). Repeat with the remaining eggs.

Line a baking sheet with baking parchment. Beat the remaining 2 eggs in a shallow bowl. Mix the breadcrumbs and crackling into another shallow bowl. One at a time, dip an egg into the beaten egg, shake off any excess, then coat in the breadcrumb mixture. Place on the baking sheet. Repeat with the remaining boiled eggs. Chill the sheet of eggs for 4 hours.

Fill a deep pan one-third full with sunflower oil, and heat to 170°C (or until a cube of bread sizzles and turns golden in 1 minute). Cooking about 2 eggs at a time, carefully add the eggs to the hot oil, cook for about 6–8 minutes, turning once, until golden and crispy. Using a slotted spoon, remove the eggs onto kitchen paper to drain. Check the oil temperature, then repeat with the remaining eggs. Best eaten on the day.

MAKES 8

85g butter, cold and cubed, plus extra to grease
350g self-raising flour, plus more for dusting
1 teaspoon baking powder
½ teaspoon mustard powder
¼ teaspoon salt
125g strong Cheddar cheese, coarsely grated
65g ham, torn into small pieces
50g Snaffling Pig Ham & Coleman's Mustard Crackling, roughly crushed
175ml buttermilk
1 medium egg, beaten, to glaze

CHEESE & HAM SCONES

These are delicious served warm with soup, or even as breakfast on the go. You can use whatever cheese you like in these, but we think the strong Cheddar goes really well with the Ham & Coleman's crackling.

Preheat the oven to 220°C/200°C Fan/Gas Mark 7. Grease a baking sheet and put it in the oven to heat up. Sift the flour, baking powder and mustard powder into a large bowl, add the salt and mix. Add the butter, then lightly rub in with your fingertips until the mixture looks like breadcrumbs.

Stir 100g of the Cheddar, the ham and crackling into the flour mix, being careful not to overmix and break up the crackling too much. Make a well in the dry mix, pour in the buttermilk and combine it quickly with a cutlery knife until the dough comes together.

Sprinkle some flour onto the work surface and tip the dough out. Flour the dough and your hands with a little more flour, then knead the dough a little until smooth (the key to good scones is not to overwork the dough, so go lightly).

Pat into a round, about 4cm deep. Flour a serrated knife and cut the dough into 8 wedges. Brush the tops with beaten egg and sprinkle with the remaining Cheddar, then carefully place each wedge onto the hot baking sheet. Bake for 12–15 minutes until risen and slightly golden. Remove and cool on a wire rack.

TOP TIP:
These are best eaten on the day they are made, but will keep for a few days in an airtight container in the fridge. To serve, warm in an oven preheated to 160°C/140°C Fan/Gas Mark 3 for a few minutes.

DO GOOD THINGS

HAVE SOME FUN

DONT BE A DICK

BEER BREAD WITH SALTED CRACKLING

MAKES 1 LOAF

60g salted butter, melted
    and cooled, plus extra
    for greasing
340g self-raising flour
1 tablespoon caster sugar
340ml beer
50g Snaffling Pig Perfectly
    Salted Crackling, roughly
    crushed

This is a very easy bread, without the need for kneading or rising, and is similar in texture to soda bread.
    You can make it with half wholegrain flour if you like, but it will be a little denser.

Preheat the oven to 180°C/160°C Fan/Gas Mark 4 and grease a 900g loaf tin with butter. Mix the flour, sugar, 50g of the melted butter and the beer, stirring until smooth (don't worry about a few lumps). Mix in half of the crackling.

Spoon the batter into the loaf tin, smoothing the top. Drizzle with the remaining 10g of melted butter and sprinkle with the remaining crackling.

Bake the bread for 45–50 minutes until a skewer inserted comes out clean. Cool on a wire rack for 5 minutes then turn out of the tin onto a wire rack to cool completely.

FISH FINGER SANDWICH

FINGER

MAKES 4 SARNIES

4 lemon sole fillets,
   skins removed
40g plain flour
2 large eggs, beaten
50g breadcrumbs
50g Snaffling Pig Salt
   & Vinegar Crackling,
   crushed to crumbs
200ml vegetable oil
8 slices of thick white bread
tartare sauce, to serve (see
   page 48 for homemade)
lemon, to squeeze
50g rocket, to serve

Comfort food heaven: the fish finger
sandwich has had a gourmet update in
recent years and is often found on the menu
of gastro pubs. We think lemon sole works
best to give a really soft flaky fish finger,
and a good white loaf is a must!

Slice the fish fillets into about 16 strips of fish. Into 3 separate
bowls put the flour, the beaten egg and finally the breadcrumbs and
crackling crumbs. Dip the fish first into the flour (tap off excess), then
the egg (tap off excess) and finally the crumbs to coat.

Heat half of the oil in a large frying pan. Fry half of the fish fingers for
3 minutes, turning once, until golden. Drain on kitchen paper. Discard
any oil in the pan, then wipe the pan clean with kitchen paper. Repeat
with the remaining oil and fish fingers.

Spread the bread with tartare sauce, squeeze the lemon over the
rocket leaves, then assemble the fish finger sandwiches.

CARAMELISED ONION SAUSAGE ROLLS

MAKES 10

800g sausage meat
50g breadcrumbs
a small bunch of thyme,
    leaves only
50g Snaffling Pig Low &
    Slow BBQ Crackling,
    roughly broken
500g pack puff pastry
flour, for dusting
6 tablespoons
    caramelised
    onion chutney
1 egg, beaten
2 teaspoons sesame
    seeds

These make hearty-sized sausage rolls, the perfect bar snack, we think. The crackling in these melts slightly, adding a delicious BBQ flavour to the sausage meat.

Preheat the oven to 200°C/180°C Fan/Gas Mark 6. Line 2 baking sheets with baking parchment. In a medium bowl mix together the sausage meat, breadcrumbs, thyme and crackling.

Cut the pastry block in half, and roll each block on a lightly floured surface into a 23cm x 32cm strip. Divide the chutney between the 2 strips and spread lengthways along the middle of the pastry, leaving a 3cm border on both of the long edges. Divide the sausage meat into 2 and place along each line of chutney.

Brush the long borders with a little egg, and fold the pastry over on both pastry strips, to encase the sausage meat. Seal the edges with a fork, making a pattern along the edges. Slice each roll into 5, brush each roll with a little egg and sprinkle over the sesame seeds. Arrange on the baking sheets. Bake for 30—35 minutes until golden and the sausage is cooked through.

WELSH RAREBIT

The crackling in this classic dish adds a delicious crunch and rich flavour. Let the mixture cool slightly before topping the bread, to make it easier to use.

In a small pan heat the stout, then stir in the cheese until mostly melted. Remove from the heat, and stir in the mustard powder, egg yolks and Worcestershire sauce. Leave to cool a little before stirring in the crackling.

Preheat the grill to high. Toast the bread on a grill rack, then spread the rarebit mixture onto the bread and grill for 2–3 minutes until golden and bubbling.

SERVES 4

3 tablespoons stout
200g strong Cheddar cheese, grated
1 teaspoon mustard powder
2 egg yolks
1 tablespoon Worcestershire sauce
20g Snaffling Pig Ham & Coleman's Mustard Crackling, crushed
4 thick slices of bread

PUNCH TAVERNS'

As we mentioned in our intro, when we started SP we knew nothing about the pub trade, other than the fact that we liked the service they provided. That meant we didn't know who Punch were. But after a few weeks of literally walking from pub to pub around where we lived, we started to realise that they were a bit of a big deal — they might not stick their name on everything but the chances are, no matter where you are in the country, one of your locals will be run by one of their lovely publicans.

Every year we do a series of roadshows with them — think of it as the equivalent to taking the band on tour, except we haven't got a tour bus, or roadies ... or groupies. OK, it's basically just us in our trusty van, aka The Hamborghini, but you get the idea. What we've discovered, though, is that if you're giving away porky samples at an event, and that event is mainly drink based, you are going to be rather popular. Who knew…?

Anyway, Chef Gabriele has worked up this beauty for us. We love the fact that it's pretty simple in terms of process (it's not like we've always got a spare hour to rustle something up in the kitchen) but as you can imagine, anything with lovely ham, a healthy dollop of melted cheese and warmed crackling topping is really pretty delicious.

...OPEN-FACED SANDWICH
WITH AUTHENTIC HOG ROAST PORK CRACKLING

This is a decadent pub sandwich, packed full of flavour. You can use ready-made caramelised onion chutney and normal softened butter if you're short on time. We like to use British-made charcuterie from Woodall's, but you can try experimenting with any cured ham you like.

The best bruschetta is a perfect mix of creamy and crunchy. The toasted sourdough bread base, the creaminess of the Camembert paired with the cured ham, and the crunchiness of the pork scratching crumbles makes for another glorious twist on the Italian classic.

To make the garlic and parsley butter, mix the ingredients together in a small bowl. Wrap and keep in the fridge for up to 1 week.

To make the balsamic caramelised onions, in a large frying pan heat the butter and sunflower oil until melted, add the onion and some seasoning, and cook over a low heat for 15 minutes until the onion is soft. Add the sugar and turn up the heat slightly to caramelise the onions, about 5 minutes. Stir in the balsamic vinegar and bubble for 3–5 minutes until the vinegar has disappeared. It will keep in the fridge for 1 week.

Toast the sliced sourdough. Spread a quarter of the garlic butter over each slice of bread. Meanwhile, melt the rest of the garlic butter and mix it with the crumbled pork crackling, to bind. Set aside.

Preheat the grill to medium-high. Spread the caramelised onions over the sourdough slices and arrange the rocket leaves on both slices.

Lay the ham slices over the rocket leaves and top with enough Camembert so that the cheese covers most of the bread. Place the bread under the grill to lightly melt the cheese. Reheat the pork crackling crumble.

Sprinkle over the pork crackling crumble, and serve with a garden salad if you like.

SERVES 2–4
[DEPENDING ON HOW HUNGRY YOU ARE!]

2 slices of sourdough bead
15g garlic and parsley butter (see below)
20g Snaffling Pig Authentic Perfectly Salted Crackling (or flavour of your choice), roughly crumbled
15g balsamic caramelised onions (see below)
wild rocket leaves, to serve
2 slices of cured ham
4 slices of English Camembert cheese, sliced 5mm thick

FOR THE GARLIC AND PARSLEY BUTTER
50g butter, softened
1 large garlic clove, crushed
1 tablespoon chopped curly parsley

FOR THE BALSAMIC CARAMELISED ONIONS
15g butter
1 teaspoon sunflower oil
1 red onion, sliced
1 teaspoon brown sugar
1 tablespoon balsamic vinegar
salt and pepper, to season

CRACKLING ONION RINGS

Perfect as a snack with beer, or stuffed inside a burger. These can even be reheated in an oven if they don't all get snaffled at once — unlikely, though!

Peel and slice the onions into rounds about 1.5cm thick. Put the flour on a large plate. Whisk the eggs together in a shallow bowl. Mix the breadcrumbs and crackling together in another bowl.

Working in small batches, toss the onion rings in the flour, then dip in the egg, followed by the breadcrumb and crackling mixture to coat. Lay on a baking sheet lined with parchment paper, while you coat the remaining onion rings.

Fill a high-sided pan one-third full with the oil, and heat to 190°C (or until a pinch of the breadcrumbs browns in 30 seconds). Fry the onions in 3 or 4 batches for 2 minutes, until golden. Scoop out with a slotted spoon and drain on kitchen paper. Serve immediately.

STARTERS

#DREAMPIG

THE Snaffling Pig co.

AWESOME FLAVOURED

PORK CRACKLING

LET'S MAKE THE PIGGIN' MAGIC HAPPEN

TROT TO TROT HABA

CRA

AWESO

PORK

THE Snaffling Pig co.
PERFECTLY
CRAFTED BY THE BREWER PIG
the Snaffling Pig co
FLAVOURED
CRACKLING

SALT & VINEGAR FISH CAKES

MAKES 8

450g floury potatoes
450g cod fillets
300g can marrowfat
    peas, drained
2 tablespoons tartare sauce
    (see page 48 for homemade)
1 tablespoon malt vinegar
40g plain flour
2 eggs, beaten
100g panko breadcrumbs,
    or use regular breadcrumbs
    if you like
75g Snaffling Pig Salt & Vinegar
    Crackling, roughly crushed
175ml sunflower oil, to fry
salt and pepper, to season

Our fishcakes are a nod to the local chippy: cod, salt and vinegar chips and mushy peas all wrapped up in an easy to make fishcake! These also work well as a mid-week meal.

Peel and chop the potatoes into even-size chunks, put into a large pan and cover with cold water. Cover with a lid and bring to the boil, then simmer for 10 minutes. Add the cod and continue cooking for 5 minutes. Carefully remove the fish, and remove the skin (if present) and set aside. Drain the potatoes and steam dry for 1 minute.

Tip the potatoes into a large bowl, and mash. Stir in the peas, tartare sauce and vinegar, and plenty of salt to season. Gently stir in the cod flakes. Shape into 8 patties, arrange on a baking sheet and chill for 30 minutes.

Arrange the flour in a shallow bowl, the beaten egg in another shallow bowl, and finally mix the breadcrumbs and crackling together in a final bowl. One at a time, dip the fishcakes in the flour (tap off excess), dip in the egg (drain off excess), then coat in the breadcrumb mixture. Chill the fishcakes if you like, or fry immediately.

In a large frying pan, heat the oil over a medium heat and fry the fishcakes for 3–5 minutes each side until golden (in batches if necessary). Drain on kitchen paper and serve immediately.

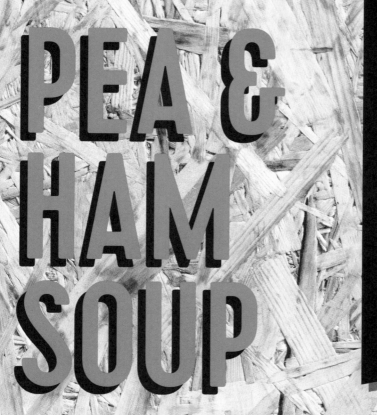

PEA & HAM SOUP

SERVES 6
[OR 4 AS A MAIN]

50g butter
1 large onion, finely
   chopped
1 garlic clove, crushed
1 litre hot chicken stock
600g gammon steaks
900g frozen peas
a small bunch of mint
   (plus extra to serve)
crème fraîche, to serve
extra virgin olive oil,
   to drizzle
50g Snaffling Pig Ham
   & Coleman's Mustard
   Crackling
salt and pepper,
   to season

Our Ham & Coleman's Crackling is a match made in heaven with this vibrant soup. Using gammon steaks makes this a hearty soup worthy of a winter's lunch.

Heat the butter in a large pan and fry the onion for 10 minutes until soft; add the garlic for 1 minute. Add the chicken stock and bring to the boil. Add the gammon steaks, cover, and simmer for 5–7 minutes until cooked through.

Remove the gammon with a slotted spoon and set aside on a board. Add 800g of the peas and the mint, bring back to the boil and simmer for 2 minutes. Let it cool for 5 minutes, remove the mint sprigs, then blend with a stick blender or transfer to a blender.

Meanwhile, shred the gammon into fine pieces, discarding any fat. Return the soup to the pan, reheat, and add the shredded gammon and remaining peas. Add seasoning if required. Divide among 6 warmed soup bowls, and swirl with crème fraîche and a little oil. Garnish with the crackling and some mint leaves.

CRISPY SCAMPI

SERVES 4

175g plain flour
40g cornflour
150ml fridge-cold lager
100g Snaffling Pig Perfectly Salted Crackling, crushed
15–20 peeled scampi tails, or raw king prawns
sunflower oil, to fry

FOR THE TARTARE SAUCE
125g mayonnaise
2 tablespoons capers, rinsed and chopped
2 gherkins, finely chopped
a pinch of sugar
2 tablespoons finely chopped parsley
1 tablespoon finely chopped tarragon

You can get scampi tails from fishmongers or online, otherwise use good-quality king prawns. The crackling in these add extra crunch to the prawns; try using our Habanero Crackling next time for added spice!

Make the batter by mixing together 125g of the plain flour and the cornflour together in a large bowl; gradually stir in the lager, creating a smooth batter that coats the spoon (add a little more flour or lager as necessary).

Mix together the tartare sauce ingredients and set aside.

Fill a high-sided pan one-third full with the oil, and heat to 190°C (or until a cube of bread sizzles and turns golden in 30 seconds). Put the remaining 50g of flour into a shallow bowl. Place the crackling in a separate bowl. In batches, dip the scampi/prawns in the flour to coat, then dip into the batter, followed by the crackling. Carefully drop into the hot oil and fry until golden and floating. Scoop out and drain on kitchen paper, then repeat with the remaining scampi. Serve with the tartare sauce.

LET'S MAKE THE
PIGGIN' MAGIC HAPPEN
LOW & SLOW BBQ
HOT TO
MARVELLOUS

SERVES 6
[OR 4 AS A MAIN]

750g sweet potatoes
2 red onions, sliced in wedges
6 tablespoons olive oil
2 teaspoons ground cinnamon
200g cooked puy lentils
1 red chilli, finely sliced
50g rocket
3 tablespoons pomegranate
   molasses
juice of ½ lemon
4 tablespoons pomegranate
   seeds
150g feta
30g Snaffling Pig Habanero
   Crackling, roughly broken
salt and pepper, to season

SWEET POTATO SALAD

WITH LENTILS, POMEGRANATE AND PORK CRACKLING CROUTONS

We think our crackling makes great croutons, and can be added to all sorts of salads. The Habanero Crackling really peps up this elegant salad.

To reduce the carb content in this salad you could swap the sweet potatoes for peeled and chopped celeriac and replace the pomegranate molasses with the juice of 1 lemon.

Preheat the oven to 200°C/180°C Fan/Gas Mark 6. Chop the sweet potatoes into 2.5cm pieces (leaving the skin on) and put into a roasting tin with the onion. Drizzle with 2 tablespoons of the oil and sprinkle over 1 teaspoon of the cinnamon and some seasoning. Roast for 20–25 minutes until the potatoes are tender and beginning to char.

Mix the sweet potato and onion with the lentils, chilli and rocket in a large salad bowl. In a separate bowl mix together the remaining 4 tablespoons of oil, the remaining teaspoon of cinnamon, and the pomegranate molasses and lemon juice. Toss the salad with the dressing, and scatter over the pomegranate seeds, feta and crackling croutons.

ULTIMATE CAESAR SALAD

WITH CRACKLING CROUTONS

Charring the baby gem adds so much flavour to the salad, and we think the crackling is a much better substitution for your run-of-the-mill crouton! This is a great low-carb recipe.

Begin by making the dressing. Finely chop the anchovies until they become a paste. Place in a small bowl and mix in the mayonnaise, garlic, Parmesan and lemon juice. Set aside.

Carefully slice the tip off the end of each of the lettuces (keeping the heart intact so they hold their shape), and slice each in half lengthways.

Heat a griddle/frying pan. Brush the cut side of the lettuces with 2 tablespoons of the oil, and griddle/fry for 1 minute until they begin to char. Arrange on a platter.

Put the chicken between 2 sheets of baking parchment, and bash with a rolling pin to flatten slightly. Rub the chicken fillets with the remaining oil and season, then griddle/fry for 4–5 minutes each side. Remove, and slice into strips. Add to the lettuce along with the tomatoes. Drizzle with the dressing and scatter over the Parmesan shavings and crackling. Season well and serve with extra lemon wedges.

SERVES 4
[OR 2 FOR A FILLING LUNCH]

6 baby gem lettuces
3 tablespoons olive oil
2 skinless chicken
   breast fillets
75g sundried tomatoes,
   drained and roughly
   chopped
Parmesan shavings
50g Snaffling Pig Perfectly
   Salted Crackling
salt and pepper, to season
lemon wedges, to serve

FOR THE DRESSING
4 anchovy fillets in
   oil, drained
150g mayonnaise
1 garlic clove, crushed
3 tablespoons finely
   grated Parmesan
2 tablespoons lemon juice

WE'RE NOT ONES FOR BIG, GUSHY VALUE STATEMENTS, BUT WE'VE GOT OUR THREE SIMPLE RULES ⟶

WE THINK THEY DO THE PIGGIN' TRICK

DO GREAT THINGS

HAVE SOME FUN

DON'T BE A DICK

MAINS

B & K'S

Brewhouse and Kitchen (or B&K as we'll now call them) will always have a place close to our heart at SP, as they were one of the very first pub groups to take our porky wares beyond the areas we lived in. In fact they took us all the way down to the lovely land that is Poole. Bless their (no doubt trendy) cotton socks.

But when we visited them, we realised they were much more than just pork snack trail blazers — because this lot brew their own beer at each site (granted, given their name we might have guessed that). It's not kept in a shed or locked away from prying eyes either — if you've been to one you'll know it's very much a central part of the pub. As a concept, it is, in our opinion, bad ass, which is a technical term.

Chef Tom is the keeper of all things food at B&K and for his recipe, he's dialling up the porky factor to the power of three, all wrapped up in the bun-based perfection that is a burger. You'll see we've added some natty comedy flags to ours; feel free to leave them out if you're following a low-pun lifestyle.

THREE LITTLE PIGGIES BURGER

SERVES 6

FOR THE BURGERS
400g minced beef
200g minced pork
½ small onion, finely chopped
1 medium egg yolk
2 teaspoons Dijon mustard
1 gherkin, finely chopped
50g Snaffling Pig Low & Slow
    BBQ Crackling, crushed
    to breadcrumbs
50g breadcrumbs
3 tablespoons sunflower oil

TO ASSEMBLE
6 brioche burger buns
6 slices of Cheddar cheese
½ cos lettuce, sliced
2 tomatoes, sliced
1 red onion, sliced
3 gherkins, halved
pulled pork (see page 75)
Snaffling Pig Ham & Coleman's
    Crackling, roughly crushed

Nothing beats a proper burger, and we think ours takes a lot of beating. You can use all beef if you like, but the pork adds a lot of flavour, and feel free to use different flavoured crackling.

To reduce the carb content in these burgers substitute the breadcrumbs with the same amount of crushed crackling, and serve the burgers with a salad rather than in a bun.

Put everything for the burgers (except the oil) into a non-metallic bowl and mix. Cover and chill for 1 hour.

Using wet hands, divide the mince mixture into 6 and shape into patties. Heat the oil in a large pan, and fry the burgers for 5–8 minutes each side, until browned and cooked through.

Meanwhile heat the grill to medium-high, halve the brioche buns and toast the cut sides under the grill until golden. Top each burger with a slice of cheese, and put it under the grill until it is melted and has started to bubble. Serve the burgers with the lettuce, tomatoes, onions, gherkins and a generous helping of pulled pork. Top with crushed crackling and there you have it — three little pigs!

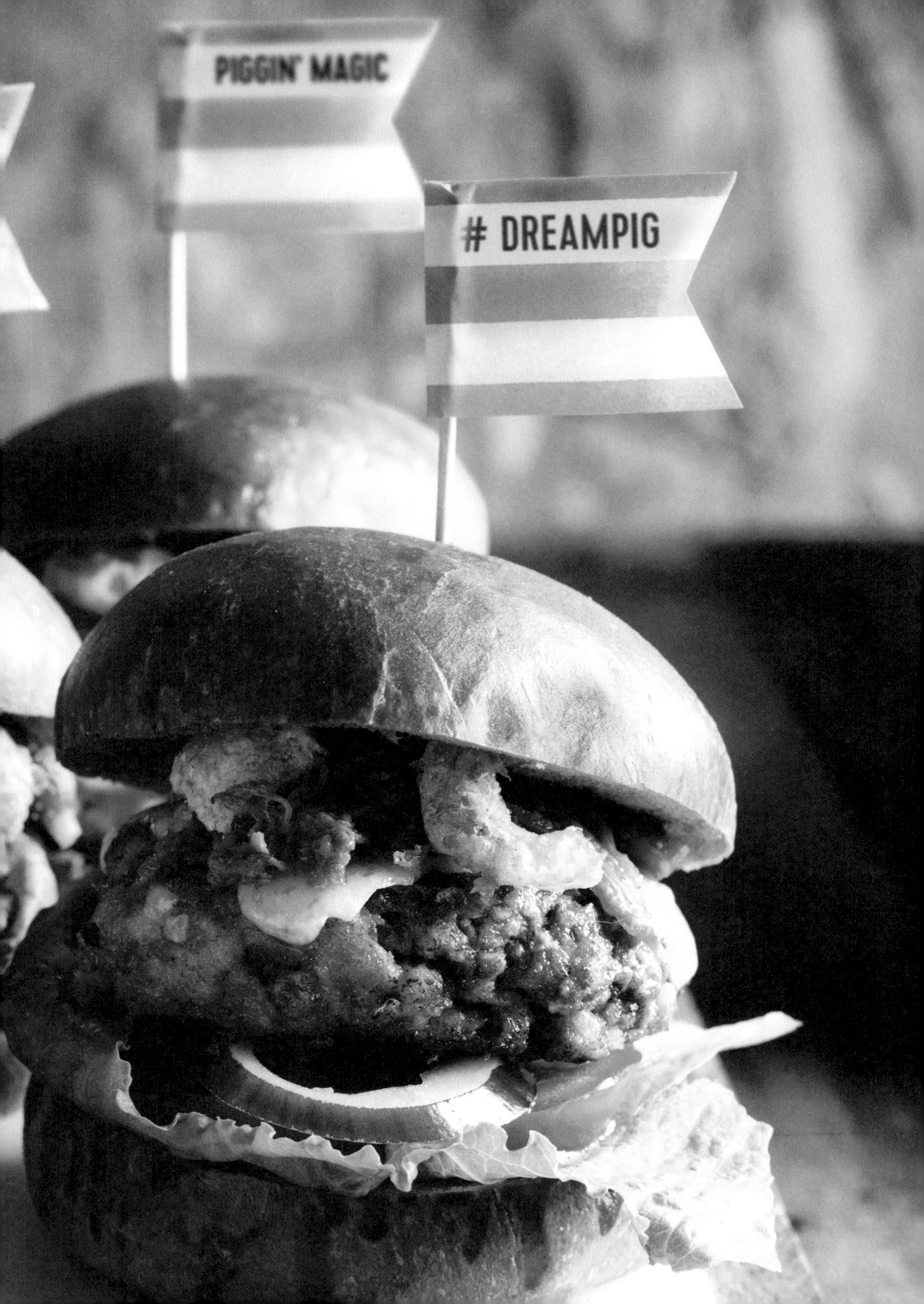
PIGGIN' MAGIC
DREAMPIG

PAD THAI

SERVES 4

300g flat rice noodles
2 tablespoons vegetable oil
300g chicken breast, cut
    into thin strips
300g raw tiger prawns,
    tails left on if you can
    find them
5 spring onions, thinly sliced
200g beansprouts
25g salted peanuts, finely
    chopped
30g Snaffling Pig Perfectly
    Salted Crackling,
    roughly broken
a small bunch of coriander,
    roughly chopped

FOR THE TAMARIND SAUCE

75g dark brown sugar
4 tablespoons tamarind
    paste
50ml fish sauce
juice of 1 lime, plus wedges
    to serve

This delicious Thai-influenced dish is full of sweet, sour and salty flavour, and we've added our crackling in with the peanuts for extra crunch and meaty flavour. If you want to add some heat, why not use the Habanero Crackling?

Prepare the noodles, according to the pack instructions. Mix together the tamarind sauce ingredients in a small bowl.

In a large frying pan or wok, heat the oil, add the chicken and fry for 5–8 minutes until cooked through. Add the prawns, spring onions and beansprouts, and fry for a few minutes until the prawns turn pink.

Stir in the noodles, followed by the tamarind sauce, and bubble for 1 minute until everything is coated. Scatter over the peanuts, crackling and coriander, and serve with lime wedges.

900g floury potatoes
    (medium sized)
25g butter, plus extra to
    grease
2 onions, sliced
1 garlic clove, crushed
300ml double cream
300ml milk
1½ tablespoons
    wholegrain mustard
a small bunch of thyme
150g shredded ham hock
50g Snaffling Pig Ham
    & Coleman's Mustard
    Crackling
salt and pepper, to
    season

HAM HOCK & POTATO BAKE

This is a delicious mid-week meal served with a mustardy salad; or you could serve it as a side alongside a roast.

Preheat the oven to 180°C/160°C Fan/Gas Mark 4. Peel the potatoes, and slice thinly. Melt the butter in a large saucepan, add the onion and fry over a medium heat for 10 minutes until soft. Add the garlic and cook for a further minute.

Add the cream and milk and bring to the boil, turn down to a simmer, add the potatoes and simmer, covered, for 10–15 minutes until the potatoes begin to soften and the cream thickens. Stir in the mustard, seasoning and most of the thyme.

Lightly butter an ovenproof dish, spoon in half of the potatoes, scatter over the ham hock and half of the crackling, then layer up the remaining potatoes and finish with the remaining crackling. Cover the dish with foil and bake for 45 minutes. Remove the foil and continue baking for 15–20 minutes until golden on top. Let it sit for 10 minutes, then slice and scatter over the remaining thyme.

HAM, EGG & PORK CRACKLING CHIPS

SERVES 2

2 large potatoes
4 tablespoons sunflower oil
40g Snaffling Pig Low & Slow
    BBQ Crackling, crushed
    to crumbs
2 large eggs
2 thick slices of ham
    or leftover gammon
piccalilli or ketchup,
    to serve

The crackling seasons these chips and makes them extra crunchy. They are delicious with a fried egg and a thick slice of ham for a quick dinner.

Preheat the oven to 200°C/180°C Fan/Gas Mark 6. Cut the potatoes into thick chips (leaving the skin on), and place in a large pan of water. Bring to the boil and simmer for 5 minutes, until they have tender edges. Drain and steam dry for 5 minutes.

Meanwhile put 3 tablespoons of the oil into a large baking sheet and heat in the oven for 5 minutes. Add the chips to the hot oil, then sprinkle over the crackling and turn to coat. Cook for 35–40 minutes.

When the chips are nearly cooked, heat the remaining oil in a large frying pan and fry the eggs for a few minutes. Serve the chips with the ham and eggs, and piccalilli or ketchup if you like.

PEPPERONI CRACKLING

PIZZA

Yes, you can even put crackling into a pizza base; just make sure it's small enough so it doesn't tear the dough when you roll it out. It adds a lovely crunchy texture!

Pizza dough is simple and quick to make, so it's ideal for a Friday night. Double the recipe to make 2 pizzas if you like.

In a large bowl mix together the flour, yeast, semolina and a pinch of salt. Make a well in the centre, add the oil and 100ml of warm water, and mix to make a soft dough. Tip out and knead briefly. Grease the bowl with some oil and put the dough inside; cover with a tea towel and rest for 30 minutes.

Grease a baking sheet with oil and sprinkle with a little semolina. Preheat the oven to 240°C/220°C Fan/Gas Mark 9. Tip the dough out on to a lightly floured surface, knead in half of the crackling, then roll out to a 30cm circle.

Transfer the dough to the baking sheet. Spread over the pizza sauce, scatter over the mozzarella, pepperoni and remaining crackling, and season with some pepper. Bake for 12–15 minutes until the dough is crisp and the cheese is bubbling. Scatter with some basil leaves to serve.

150g strong white flour, plus extra to dust
½ teaspoon fast-action dried yeast
½ tablespoon semolina, plus extra to dust
1 tablespoon extra virgin olive oil, plus extra to grease
50g Snaffling Pig Habanero Crackling, lightly crushed to small pieces
4 tablespoons tomato pizza sauce
100g mozzarella cheese, torn into small pieces
75g pepperoni slices
basil leaves, to serve
salt and pepper, to season

BAKED FISH WITH TOMATO & BUTTERBEANS

SERVES 4

4 tablespoons olive oil
125g chorizo, diced
2 garlic cloves, crushed
2 tablespoons tomato purée
500g cherry tomatoes
1 tablespoon sherry vinegar
2 teaspoons caster sugar
400g can butterbeans,
    drained and rinsed
50g breadcrumbs
50g Snaffling Pig Habanero
    Crackling, crushed
finely grated zest of 1 small
    lemon, plus wedges to
    serve
a small bunch of parsley,
    roughly chopped
4 cod fillets, skin removed

This summery Spanish dish is spiced up with our Habanero Crackling but if you're not keen on spice, why not try using the BBQ flavour instead?
  You can use any firm white fish you like for this dish.

Preheat the oven to 220°C/200°C Fan/Gas Mark 7. Heat 1 tablespoon of the oil in a large frying pan and fry the chorizo until golden and releasing its oil, about 5 minutes. Add 1 crushed garlic clove and the tomato purée, and cook for 1 minute.

Stir in the cherry tomatoes, vinegar, sugar and 100ml of water and cook for 10 minutes until the tomatoes are beginning to break down. Stir in the butterbeans, then transfer to an ovenproof dish.

In a small bowl make the crumb. Mix together the breadcrumbs, remaining garlic, crackling, lemon zest, most of the parsley and the remaining 3 tablespoons of oil. Press the crumb mixture on top of the cod fillets, then arrange the fish on top of the butterbean mixture. Bake in the oven for 15–20 minutes, until the crumb is golden and the fish is cooked. Sprinkle with the remaining parsley before serving.

SERVES 8

2 teaspoons sweet smoked paprika
3 tablespoons light brown sugar
½ tablespoon mustard powder
a sprig of thyme, leaves picked
2 tablespoons oil
1 onion, sliced
1.8kg boneless pork shoulder, skin removed
250ml cider
8 brioche buns, split
apple sauce (see page 20 for homemade)
100g Snaffling Pig Perfectly Salted Crackling
salt and pepper, to season

PULLED PORK BUNS WITH CRACKLING

This is such an easy recipe for when you've got a crowd of people over, and you can let people serve themselves. Using our crackling means you don't need to worry about making the skin of your pork crispy.

To reduce the carb content in this recipe you could serve the pulled pork with a salad, rather than in a bun.

Preheat the oven to 220°C/200°C Fan/Gas Mark 7. In a small bowl mix together the paprika, sugar, mustard powder, thyme, oil and plenty of seasoning. Put the onion in a roasting tin just big enough to hold the pork, sit the pork on top and rub the pork with the oil mix. Roast in the oven for 30 minutes to brown. Remove the roasting tin from the oven, and turn the oven down to 150°C/130°C Fan/Gas Mark 2.

Carefully pour the cider around, not on top of, the pork. Cover the tin tightly with foil, and cook in the oven for 5 hours, or until the meat can easily be shredded with 2 forks.

Remove the pork from the tin, shred it onto a platter and drizzle over the tin juices. Fill the buns with the pulled pork, apple sauce and some crackling.

ULTIMATE MAC & CHEESE

SERVES 4–6

125g butter
2 leeks, finely sliced
75g bacon lardons
400g macaroni pasta
100g plain flour
1 teaspoon mustard powder
200ml pale ale
1 litre whole milk
150g strong Cheddar
 cheese, coarsely grated
125g Gruyère cheese,
 coarsely grated
2 tablespoons chopped
 chives
75g Snaffling Pig Low &
 Slow BBQ Crackling
salt and pepper, to season

We've added bacon and beer to our Mac and Cheese – this has to be the ultimate comfort dinner! You can use whichever crackling you like to top it, but we think the BBQ is a winner.

Heat 25g of the butter in a large frying pan, and gently fry the leeks until soft, about 10 minutes. Add the lardons and fry for 5 minutes until turning crisp. Set aside. Bring a large pan of water to the boil; cook the macaroni for 5–8 minutes until just tender, then drain.

Meanwhile preheat the grill to medium-high. Melt the remaining 100g of butter in a large pan, stir in the flour and mustard powder, and cook for 1 minute. Remove the pan from the heat, and gradually stir in the beer followed by the milk.

Return the pan to the heat, and bring to the boil, stirring constantly, until the sauce is thickened. Stir in most of the cheese and chives, followed by the leek mixture and cooked pasta, season to taste. Pour into an ovenproof dish. Scatter over the crackling and remaining cheese and chives, and grill for 5–10 minutes until golden and bubbling.

RETURN
OF THE MAC

YOUNG'S

Our friends at Young's don't mess about when it comes to food — if you've been in one of their pubs you'll know that a lot of them have open kitchens, complete with obligatory scary-looking head chef. Don't worry — we've met a lot of them, and they're all lovely really, which means you absolutely can give them an intense 'give me the biggest yorkie pud' stare if you're watching them plate up your Sunday roast. If you're still a bit worried, one of us actually has a Young's pub at the end of his road, so we'll give it a go and report back on the pud-to-plate ratio.

Recipe wise, Chef Wayne and his team went big and came up with not one, but two recipes (see page 110 for their cheesecake) that follow his ethos of seasonal British produce. Hurrah. Having tried everything we can confirm they are both frankly excellent, and as there's a savoury and sweet option you have a full meal of Young's-based swine dining whenever you want.

...FRIED CHICKEN ON POTATO WAFFLE

WITH MAPLE GRAVY AND HABANERO CRACKLING CRUMB

Fried chicken on waffles may seem a little odd, but it's bang on trend at the moment and for good reason — don't knock it until you've tried it! You can keep everything warm until ready to serve.

To prepare the chicken, in a medium bowl mix together the buttermilk, lime zest and juice and some seasoning. Add the chicken and mix to coat. Cover the bowl and leave to marinate in the fridge for at least 1 hour (overnight is best).

Meanwhile, make the waffles. In a large bowl sift the flour and baking powder together, then mix in the mashed potato. Beat in the eggs and milk until smooth, then add the chives and some seasoning. Brush a waffle iron with a little oil, and heat according to the manufacturer's instructions. Fill the waffle maker with some of the batter and cook until crisp. Keep warm while you make the remaining waffles.

Mix the habanero crumb with the breadcrumbs. Remove the chicken from the marinade one piece at a time (keeping as much of the buttermilk coating on the chicken as possible), and coat in the crumb mixture. Place on a tray whilst you coat the remaining chicken.

Fill a high-sided pan one-third full with oil, and heat to 160°C. Fry the chicken in batches for 8–10 minutes until golden, and the chicken is cooked.

Meanwhile make the gravy. In a small pan boil the chicken stock until reduced by one-third, add the chilli flakes and maple syrup, bring to the boil and remove from the heat.

To serve, place the chicken fillets on top of the waffles, and garnish with the coriander leaves, lime wedges, pickled chillies and a drizzle of the maple gravy.

SERVES 4

FOR THE CHICKEN
120ml buttermilk
2 limes, zest and juice
300g chicken breast fillets, chopped into large pieces
50g Snaffling Pig Habanero Crackling, crushed to crumbs
150g panko breadcrumbs, or use regular breadcrumbs if you like
sunflower oil, to deep fry

FOR THE WAFFLES
85g plain flour
½ teaspoon baking power
250g cold mashed potato
4 large eggs
100ml milk
1 tablespoon chopped chives
oil, to fry

FOR THE GRAVY
400ml chicken stock
1 teaspoon chilli flakes
100ml maple syrup
salt and pepper, to season

TO SERVE
coriander leaves
lime wedges
25g pickled chillies

SERVES 3–4

75ml sunflower oil
6 sausages
1 tablespoon picked
    thyme leaves
50g Snaffling Pig Ham
    & Coleman's Mustard
    Crackling, roughly
    crushed

FOR THE YORKSHIRE PUDDING BATTER
225g plain flour
a pinch of salt
3 eggs
1 egg white
300–375ml milk

FOR THE ONION GRAVY
75g butter
3 onions, sliced
1 teaspoon soft brown
    sugar
1½ tablespoons flour
600ml beef or chicken
    stock
a small bunch of thyme

TOAD IN THE HOLE

There is nothing more British than toad in the hole, and the crackling takes this to the next level. Make sure to let your batter rest, as this helps it to rise and guarantees you lots of oooohs and ahhhs as you pull it out the oven.

Begin by making the batter. In a large bowl sift the flour and stir in the salt, make a well in the middle then add the eggs and egg white, followed by the milk, whisking all the time. Pour into a large jug, cover and rest for 1 hour (or longer in the fridge). Add a little milk to loosen if needed after resting.

Preheat the oven to 220°C/200°C Fan/Gas Mark 7. Pour the oil in a large roasting dish (about 20 x 30cm), add the sausages and cook in the oven for 15 minutes until the sausages are browned.

Carefully remove the sausage pan from the oven, and pour in the batter; quickly sprinkle over the thyme and crackling, and cook for about 40 minutes, until puffed and golden.

Meanwhile, make the gravy. Heat the butter and fry the onions for about 20 minutes, until golden. Add the sugar and continue cooking for 5 minutes, then add the flour and cook for 1 minute. Gradually add the stock, stirring often, until smooth. Add the thyme, bring the gravy to the boil and simmer for about 5 minutes, until thickened.

Serve the gravy alongside the toad in the hole.

PIG IN THE
HOLE

PORK BAO BUNS

These Chinese steamed buns are much easier to make then they look, and are incredibly moreish. Use leftover pulled pork to stuff them, or you can buy ham hock in most supermarkets. The crackling works really well with the softness of the buns, so keep the pieces fairly large.

In a large bowl mix together the flour, yeast and sugar. In a jug mix together the vinegar, milk and 175ml of warm water. Make a well in the dry mixture, pour in the liquid, and stir quickly to make a smooth dough. Tip the dough onto a floured surface and knead for 10–15 minutes until it springs back when pushed. Put it into a large oiled bowl, and cover the bowl with clingfilm. Leave to rise for 1½ hours until doubled in size. Cut out twelve 10cm squares of baking parchment.

Tip the dough onto a floured surface and knead in the baking powder. Divide into 12 balls, and roll out each dough ball with a rolling pin into an oval about 3mm thick. Top each piece of dough with a square of baking parchment, and fold each oval in half (so the paper is the middle). Place the buns in a roasting tin lined with baking parchment and loosely cover with clingfilm. Leave to rise for 30–45 minutes until doubled in size.

Meanwhile, mix the carrot with the vinegar and sugar, and set aside to marinate for 30 minutes. In a small pan mix together the BBQ sauce and ham hock/pulled pork and a splash of water to loosen, then simmer for 10 minutes until the pork is hot. Remove from the heat and stir though the spring onions.

Preheat a large steamer over a medium heat, carefully remove the parchment from the middle of each bun, and place the buns on top of the parchment to prevent them from sticking to the steamer. Steam the buns for about 10–12 minutes until puffed and cooked (you'll need to do them in batches). Pull the buns open, and fill with the BBQ pork, carrot pickle, radishes, coriander leaves and crackling.

BEEF PIE

Crackling makes this pastry incredibly tender and full of flavour. For all you pie connoisseurs, our entire pie is encased in pastry, not just a pastry lid! This is an involved recipe, but well worth it, we promise.

SERVES 6–8

1 tablespoon oil
1kg braising steak, chopped into 5cm pieces
50g butter
2 onions, sliced
3 carrots, peeled and chopped into large chunks
250g chestnut mushrooms, sliced
2 tablespoons tomato purée
3 tablespoons balsamic vinegar
3 tablespoons plain flour
300ml dark ale
500ml hot organic beef stock
3 sprigs of thyme, leaves picked
3 bay leaves
salt and pepper, to season

FOR THE PASTRY
550g plain flour, plus extra for dusting
100g Snaffling Pig Perfectly Salted Crackling, crushed to breadcrumbs
250g cold butter, cut into cubes, plus extra to grease
1 medium egg, beaten, to glaze

Preheat the oven to 160°C/140°C Fan/Gas Mark 3.

Make the pie filling. In a large casserole heat the oil and brown the beef in batches, remove with a slotted spoon and set aside. Add the butter, fry the onions until softened, about 10 minutes, then stir in the carrots, mushrooms, tomato purée, balsamic vinegar and flour, and cook for 1 minute. Add the beef back to the pan, along with the ale and beef stock, season well and add the herbs. Bring up to a simmer, cover with a lid, then transfer to the oven to cook for 2 hours, until the meat is meltingly tender. Remove from the oven, remove the herbs and leave to cool (you can chill this in the fridge overnight if you like).

Meanwhile make the pastry. Put the flour and crackling into a food processor, whizz to combine, then pulse in the butter until it resembles coarse breadcrumbs. Alternatively, put the flour and crackling in a large bowl and rub the butter into the flour mixture with your fingertips until it resembles coarse breadcrumbs.

Add 200ml of cold water, and mix quickly and thoroughly (or pulse in a food processor), until the pastry comes together. Knead briefly, then wrap in clingfilm, and chill in the fridge until ready to use.

To make the pie, preheat the oven to 220°C/200°C Fan/Gas Mark 7 and place a baking sheet in the oven to heat up. Roll out two-thirds of the pastry, large enough to line a 25cm spring-form tin (with excess hanging over), and carefully press into the tin. Using a slotted spoon, add the beef stew to the pie dish, leaving behind excess liquid to make a gravy later if you like.

Roll out the remaining pastry to a circle just larger than the tin. Brush the edges of the pastry with some of the egg, place the pastry lid on top, trim the excess edges, then crimp the edges to seal. Roll out the pastry remnants and cut out shapes, if you like. Stick to the pie with a little egg, then brush the pie with the egg to glaze.

Make a steam hole in the middle of the pie, then put the pie dish onto the hot baking sheet and cook for 40–45 minutes until the pastry is cooked and the filling is piping hot. Let it stand for 10 minutes before slicing.

Reheat the remaining liquid from the stew to make a gravy to serve with the pie if you like.

It took a while for us to find out about The Metropolitan Pub Company – not because we hadn't been in their pubs (it turned out we'd been in a LOT of them over the last few years), but because they tend to operate rather incognito and let their pubs do the talking – whether that be sporty chat, riverside nattering or craft beer murmurings (we're running out of talking alternatives here). There are some pretty legendary spots, including a pub called The Square Pig, which, as you can imagine, is our kind of place.

But what we're talking about here is food, obvs. And, that's when our man Chef Arthur comes into his element. It's fair to say he's pushed the piggin' boat out with this recipe, which if you're feeling adventurous has the steps to make almost everything from scratch – when he first sent it over there was a lot of beard stroking and nodding of approval from our team. If we're honest, this one would be amazing without our porky wares gracing the top of it, but we'd like to think of ourselves as a crunchy, fried cherry on top of Chef's rather special tostadas.

As an extra geeky note, while there are Caribbean flavours flowing through this, the tostada is very much a South American dish and is particularly linked to Mexico. And that's pretty apt, as our Mexican cousins LOVE a porky snack (maybe even more than we do in the UK) and it's reckoned they eat more chicharrón than anywhere else in the world. Anyway, here endeth the piggin' geography lesson, over to Chef...

METRO PUB'S
CARIBBEAN JERK PORK TOSTADAS

SERVES 6

FOR THE PORK
1 tablespoon jerk seasoning
½ teaspoon curry powder
½ teaspoon cayenne pepper
1.25kg pork belly

FOR THE PICKLED ONIONS
100ml red wine vinegar
¼ teaspoon coriander seeds
¼ teaspoon mustard seeds
¼ teaspoon whole fenugreek
2 tablespoons caster sugar
½ red onion, thinly sliced

FOR THE SPICED BBQ RUM SAUCE
2 tablespoons oil
1 large onion, finely chopped
1 garlic clove, crushed
1 tablespoon smoked paprika
80g soft brown sugar
50ml white wine vinegar
100ml spiced rum
500ml passata

FOR THE PINEAPPLE SALSA
1 tablespoon butter
½ pineapple, chopped into large fingers
3 beef tomatoes, deseeded and roughly chopped
½ cucumber, deseeded and roughly chopped
1 apple, cored and roughly chopped

TO ASSEMBLE
8 corn tortillas
2 teaspoons crumbled feta
50g Snaffling Pig Habanero Crackling
coriander, optional

This has quite a few parts, but trust us, it's worth it! If you're short on time then you can just use a bought BBQ sauce.

Preheat the oven to 160°C/140°C Fan/Gas Mark 3. In a small bowl mix together the jerk seasoning with the curry powder and cayenne pepper. Put the pork belly in a roasting tin and rub over the spices. Cover the tin tightly with foil, and roast for 6 hours until meltingly tender.

Meanwhile make the pickled onions. In a small pan, heat the vinegar with the spices and sugar, and bring up to a simmer. Remove from the heat, stir and add the onion. Set aside for at least an hour.

To make the BBQ sauce, heat the oil in a medium pan and fry the onion for 5–8 minutes until soft. Stir in the garlic and paprika and cook for 1 minute. Stir ...

... in the sugar, vinegar, rum and passata and simmer for 25 minutes, until reduced and thickened. Set aside.

Meanwhile, make the pineapple salsa. Heat the butter in a large frying pan and fry the pineapple until charred on all sides, about 5 minutes. Finely chop the pineapple, and put it in a medium bowl with the tomato, cucumber and apple. Set aside.

When the pork is nearly ready, heat a large frying pan. Dry fry the tortillas one at a time, for a few minutes on both sides, until they start to puff up and catch slightly in patches. Carefully remove each tortilla from the pan with tongs and shape in a bowl or in a toast rack while it cools and sets. Repeat with the remaining tortillas.

Once the pork is tender, chop into 2cm cubes and drizzle with the BBQ sauce (alternatively you can shred the pork and toss it in the sauce). Fill the tortillas with the pork, salsa and pickled onions, and top with the feta and crackling and a final garnish of mint or coriander leaves. Serve immediately.

TOP TIPS

If you want to take it one step further, we suggest brining the pork. In a big pan, place 3–4 litres of water (or enough to cover your pork), 300g salt and 300g sugar and bring to the boil. Set aside and once cooled add the pork for 2 hours then cook as above – delish!

If you're making it, you could take your BBQ sauce up a notch and add a drop of liquid smoke, a splash of Dr Pepper and a dollop of ketchup. We also love playing around with the spices, so feel free to add Worcestershire sauce, jerk seasoning (to taste), mustard powder and some cayenne for an extra hit.

If you want a bit of extra pizzazz for your pineapple salsa and have a smoker (or BBQ that doubles as a smoker) to hand, smoke your pineapple before peeling and cutting into fingers – this is great for extracting even more flavour!

6 tablespoons extra
    virgin olive oil
zest and juice of
    1 lemon
1 teaspoon dried
    oregano
2 large garlic cloves
6 lamb cutlets
30g Snaffling Pig Salt
    & Vinegar Crackling
a small bunch of
    parsley

LAMB CHOPS

WITH GREMOLATA AND CRACKLING CRUMB

Gremolata is an Italian herby condiment and this dish is perfect when you want to make something a bit special. The lamb could also be cooked on the BBQ if the weather permits; otherwise your grill will suffice!

In a large non-metallic bowl mix together 2 tablespoons of the oil, half of the lemon juice, the oregano and 1 crushed garlic clove. Add the lamb cutlets and coat in the mixture. Marinate for 2 hours in a cool place.

To make the gremolata, put the remaining garlic, lemon zest, crackling, and parsley (leaves and stalks) into a food processor and whizz until finely chopped. Add the remaining lemon juice and olive oil to make a thick paste.

Preheat the grill to high, put the lamb cutlets onto a grill rack and grill for 2–3 minutes on each side, until done to your liking. Drizzle

LANCASHIRE HOTPOT

SERVES 6

75g butter
1kg stewing lamb, cut into
    large chunks
2 onions, sliced
3 carrots, peeled and cut
    into 5cm lengths
1 tablespoon tomato
    purée
2 tablespoons plain flour
500ml lamb stock
a few sprigs of rosemary
a small bunch of thyme
75g Snaffling Pig Perfectly
    Salted Crackling
3 large floury potatoes
    (about 900g)
salt and pepper, to season

This slow-cooked dish is perfect for a relaxed weekend at home. Let the oven take care of it and you'll have a meltingly tender hotpot to warm you up with very little effort.

To reduce the carb content in this hotpot serve the filling without the potato slices, or top with mashed celeriac instead.

Preheat the oven to 160°C/140°C Fan/Gas Mark 3. Heat 50g of the butter in a large casserole dish, brown the lamb in batches, then transfer to a plate using a slotted spoon. Brown the onions and carrots for 5–8 minutes until coloured and beginning to soften. Stir in the tomato purée and cook for 1 minute. Add the lamb back to the dish, stir in the flour and cook for 1 minute.

Add the stock, rosemary, most of the thyme and some seasoning, bring to the boil and then remove from the heat and stir in 50g of the crackling.

Peel and finely slice the potatoes. Arrange the potatoes over the stew so they are overlapping slightly. Melt the remaining butter and brush over the potatoes. Crush the remaining crackling and sprinkle onto the potatoes along with the remaining thyme leaves and some seasoning, then cover with a lid and cook for 2 hours. Remove the lid and continue cooking for 30 minutes until the potatoes are golden.

BAKED MEATBALLS

BAKED MEATBALLS

SERVES 4

125g Snaffling Pig Perfectly
  Salted Crackling, crushed
  to breadcrumbs
500g beef mince
2 heaped teaspoons Dijon
  mustard
1 tablespoon dried oregano
1 tablespoon fennel seeds
1 large egg
3 tablespoons olive oil
2 onions, sliced
2 garlic cloves, crushed
400g can chopped tomatoes
600ml passata
1 teaspoon caster sugar
1 egg yolk
250g grated mozzarella
100g mascarpone cheese
basil leaves, to serve

This comfort dish is full of robust Italian flavour and makes a great alternative to a lasagne. The crackling adds tons of meaty flavour and moisture to the meatballs.

To reduce the carb content in this dish: choose a good-quality passata without added sugar. Whilst it is a low-ish carb recipe, reducing the quantity of cheese will make it even lower.

Begin by making the meatballs. In a large bowl mix together the crackling, beef, mustard, oregano, fennel seeds and whole egg. Chill the mixture for 30 minutes to firm up. Divide the mixture into 16 golf ball-sized meatballs, place on a baking sheet, cover and chill in the fridge until needed. Preheat the oven to 190°C/170°C Fan/Gas Mark 5.

Meanwhile make the tomato sauce. Heat 2 tablespoons of the oil in a large frying pan and fry the onions until soft, about 10 minutes. Add the garlic and cook for 1 minute, followed by the chopped tomatoes, passata and sugar. Bring to the boil, then simmer uncovered for 20 minutes, stirring often.

Meanwhile put the meatballs in an ovenproof dish, drizzle with the remaining tablespoon of oil and bake in the oven for about 20 minutes, shaking the dish occasionally, until golden. In a small bowl mix together the egg yolk, 225g of the mozzarella and the mascarpone.

Spoon the tomato sauce onto the meatballs, add spoonfuls of the mascarpone mixture over the top, then scatter over the remaining mozzarella. Bake in the oven for 30 minutes, until the cheese is golden and the sauce is bubbling. Scatter with the basil and serve.

SWEETS

LET'S MAKE THE
PIGGIN' MAGIC HAPPEN
LOW & SLOW BBQ
THE Snaffling Pig co.
AWESOME FLAVOURED
PORK CRACKLING
LET'S MAKE THE
PIGGIN' MAGIC HAPPEN
SALT'N'VINEGAR
THE Snaffling Pig co.

The Snaffling Pig Co.

AWESOME FLAVOURED

PORK CRACKLING

LET'S MAKE THE
PIGGIN' MAGIC HAPPEN

MARVELLOUS MAPLE

ESOME FLAVOURED

PORK CRACKLING

LET'S MAKE THE
PIGGIN' MAGIC HAPPEN

HOT TO TROT HABANERO

#DREAM PIG

BACON BUTTER POPCORN

SERVES 6
[AS A SNACK]

1½ tablespoons vegetable oil
100g popcorn kernels
175g butter
225g caster sugar
3 tablespoons maple syrup
75g pecan halves, roughly chopped
50g Snaffling Pig Maple Crackling,
    roughly broken

Making your own toffee popcorn is so easy, and much cheaper than buying it. Make sure you use a high-sided pan, as the popcorn will expand dramatically once it starts popping. You could try this with different nuts, and different flavoured crackling too!

Heat the oil in a large pan, add the popcorn kernels, cover and cook for 3–5 minutes, shaking the pan every now and again until the popping subsides.

Empty the popcorn into a large bowl. Line 2 baking sheets with baking parchment.

Return the cleaned pan to the hob, and add the butter, sugar and maple syrup. Melt over a gentle heat, until the sugar has dissolved. Then bring to the boil, and bubble for about 5 minutes or until amber in colour; remove from the heat. Add the popcorn, pecans and crackling to the pan, and stir until everything is coated.

Spoon the popcorn mixture onto the prepared baking sheets, and leave to cool and harden. Break the popcorn up to serve.

'THAT'LL DO PIG'

MAPLE & SMOKEY BOURBON CRACKLING ICE CREAM

MAPLE & SMOKEY BOURBON CRACKLING ICE CREAM

SERVES 6

350ml whole milk
350ml double cream
5 large egg yolks
2 tablespoons sugar
220ml maple syrup
2 tablespoons bourbon
50g Snaffling Pig Maple
    Crackling, crushed to
    small pieces

This ice cream is for whisky lovers, and you can of course use whatever whisky you choose. To add smokiness to your ice cream, you can add a drop of liquid smoke (available online) to the custard for even more depth of flavour.

In a medium pan, heat the milk and cream until a few bubbles appear around the edge of the pan. Remove from the heat. In a medium bowl, mix together the egg yolks with the sugar. Gradually add the milk mixture to the yolks, stirring constantly until completely combined.

Rinse out the pan, then pour in the custard mixture. Gently heat, stirring constantly, until the custard thickens and steam rises from the surface (don't let it come to the boil). Strain back into the bowl and stir in 175ml of the maple syrup and the bourbon.

Cover the surface of the custard with clingfilm, cool to room temperature, then put in the fridge to chill completely.

Churn the chilled custard in your ice cream maker, according to the manufacturer's instructions. In a small bowl mix the crushed crackling pieces with the remaining 45ml of maple syrup, and stir though the ice cream just before it is completely frozen. Transfer to a freezer-safe container, and freeze until firm.

PECAN PIE

FOR THE PASTRY
175g plain flour, plus extra
   to dust
75g butter, cubed
   and chilled
50g icing sugar
1 medium egg

FOR THE FILLING
110g pecan halves
50g unsalted butter,
   softened
100g light soft brown sugar
3 large eggs, beaten
50g plain flour
140g maple syrup
50ml single cream
10g Snaffling Pig Maple
   Crackling, crushed
   very finely

The crackling in this pie just adds a subtle saltiness to its sticky sweetness. We love this American classic and wonder why crackling hasn't been added before!? Make sure to use proper maple syrup for maximum flavour.

To make the pastry, put the flour, butter and icing sugar into a food processor and whizz until the mixture forms fine crumbs. Alternatively, sift the flour and icing sugar into a large bowl, and rub the butter in with your fingertips.

Beat the egg with 1 teaspoon of cold water; add to the mixture and pulse/mix briefly, until the dough comes together in a ball. Wrap in clingfilm and chill for 30 minutes.

Roll the pastry on a lightly floured surface to line a 23cm fluted tart tin, and chill for 20 minutes.

Preheat the oven to 200°C/180°C Fan/Gas Mark 6. Line the pastry with baking parchment and baking beans, put the tin on a baking sheet and bake for about 15–20 minutes, until the sides are set.

Carefully remove the paper and beans, return the tart tin to the oven and bake for a further 5 minutes

Meanwhile put the pecans on a baking sheet, and toast in the oven for about 5 minutes until lightly golden, then roughly chop.

In a medium bowl beat the butter and sugar together until creamy. Gradually beat in the eggs, followed by the flour. Beat in the syrup, and then the cream.

Pour the filling mixture into the pastry case. Scatter over the pecans and crackling crumbs. Bake for 5 minutes, then lower the temperature to 180°C/160°C Fan/Gas Mark 4 and continue baking for 35–40 minutes until the filling is just set. Serve warm or at room temperature.

PECAN DO IT

MAKES 12

120ml milk
50g butter, diced
150g strong white flour,
    plus extra to dust
100g plain flour
20g caster sugar
7g fast-action dried yeast
1 medium egg
sunflower oil, to fry

FOR THE GLAZE

200g icing sugar
150ml maple syrup
30g Snaffling Pig Maple
    Crackling, roughly
    crushed

SALTED CRACKLING DOUGHNUTS

These doughnuts are crispy on the outside, with a light and airy centre. They are best eaten on the day they are made, although we don't think that will be difficult. We've glazed our doughnuts with maple icing, and a sprinkling of our salty maple crackling. They are winning!

Heat the milk in a saucepan, until bubbles just appear at the surface, then remove from the heat and mix in the butter. Leave to cool a little until lukewarm.

In a large bowl sift together the flours, stir in the sugar and yeast, then make a well. Mix the egg into the milk, pour into the well, then mix quickly to make a dough; it should be soft and slightly tacky.

On a lightly floured surface, knead the dough for about 10 minutes. Put into a lightly oiled bowl and cover with clingfilm. Leave to rise for 1½ hours, or until doubled in size.

Knead the dough lightly, then divide into 12 pieces. Roll into balls, then place the doughnuts on a large baking sheet lined with baking parchment, cover loosely with greased clingfilm, and leave to prove for 30–45 minutes until doubled in size.

When the doughnuts are nearly ready, fill a high-sided pan one-third full with some oil, and heat to 180°C.

When the doughnuts have doubled in size, working in batches use an oiled 2cm cutter to stamp out a circle in the middle of each doughnut (you can fry these later as doughnut holes!)

Fry the doughnuts in batches, for about 30 seconds–1 minute each side, until golden on both sides. Carefully remove from the oil and drain on kitchen paper, while you stamp and fry the rest.

To make the glaze, in a medium bowl mix together the icing sugar with enough maple syrup to make a spreadable glaze. Spread the glaze over the doughnuts and sprinkle with the crushed crackling. Serve warm, or at room temperature.

YOUNG'S PUB

STRAWBERRY CHEESECAKE POTS WITH CRACKLING CRUMB

This dessert is full of sweet and salty flavours. Try using Berkswell cheese if you can get hold of it; otherwise another strong sheep's cheese will do. The saltiness of the cheese works wonders with the strawberries, we promise!

SERVES 4

FOR THE COMPOTE
150g strawberries, hulled and roughly chopped, plus extra to garnish
30g icing sugar

FOR THE CHEESECAKE MIXTURE
60ml double cream
25g Berkswell cheese (or other hard sheep's cheese), finely grated
200g cream cheese
100g crème fraîche
80g sour cream
30g caster sugar
4g Snaffling Pig Pork Crackling Crumb, or use crushed salted crackling, to garnish

To make the compote, place the strawberries and icing sugar in a small pan and simmer uncovered until the strawberries have broken down.

Remove from the heat and cool.

In a small pan gently heat the double cream with most of the Berkswell cheese, to infuse. Remove from the heat and cool.

With an electric whisk, beat the cream cheese, crème fraîche, sour cream and caster sugar together. Add the infused cream and beat together until the mixture just holds its shape.

Prepare 4 glasses: put a small amount of compote into the bottom of each glass (leaving some for the top), then top with the cheesecake mixture. Chill in the fridge until ready to serve.

To serve, spoon the rest of the compote on top of each glass and garnish with a strawberry, a sprinkling of the crumb and the remaining grated cheese.

MAPLE CRACKLING BROWNIES

Bacon brownies have become a bit of a thing, and so we thought, why not try some with crackling? And we think the sweet salty combo in these ultra-rich brownies really works.

If you're a bit scared of the idea of crackling in brownies, then just scatter less of it over the top.

Preheat the oven to 180°C/160°C Fan/Gas Mark 4. Grease and line a 23 x 33cm tin. In a large bowl, beat together the eggs, cocoa, baking powder and vanilla for about 5 minutes with an electric hand whisk.

In a medium pan over a low heat, melt the butter with the sugars and maple syrup, until most of the sugar is dissolved.

Stir the butter mixture into the egg mixture, then stir in the flour, followed by the chocolate chips. Transfer to the prepared tin, and scatter over the crushed crackling.

Bake the brownies for 30 minutes, or until a crust has formed and the centre of the brownies wobbles slightly when you shake the tin. Cool completely on a wire rack. Cut when cold.

MAKES 12

225g unsalted butter, plus extra to grease
4 large eggs
100g dark cocoa powder
1 teaspoon baking powder
1 tablespoon vanilla extract
250g caster sugar
150g light brown sugar
2 tablespoons maple syrup
175g plain flour
350g dark chocolate chips
30g Snaffling Pig Maple Crackling, crushed

CRACKLING PANCAKES

Pancakes and bacon are a brunch favourite, so why not add some crackling to your next stack? Adding the crackling to the batter once the pancakes have nearly cooked stops it from going soggy, but feel free to scatter over more before serving.

In a large bowl sift together the flour and baking powder. Stir in the sugar with a pinch of salt. Make a well in the middle. In a large jug mix the eggs with the butter and milk. Pour the egg mixture into the well, and whisk into the flour.

Heat a little butter in a large frying pan, swirling the pan to coat the surface. Spoon the pancake mixture into the pan, about a small ladleful for large pancakes, or make smaller ones if you like. Cook over a medium heat, until bubbles begin to appear on the surface and the pancakes are golden underneath. Press in few pieces of crackling, flip and cook for a further minute. Keep warm in a low oven while you cook the rest.

Serve in stacks with extra crackling, some streaky bacon and a good drizzle of maple syrup.

MAKES 8 PANCAKES

250g plain flour
1 teaspoon baking powder
1 teaspoon caster sugar
a pinch of salt
2 large eggs, beaten
30g butter, melted and
    cooled, plus extra
    for cooking
275ml milk
25g Snaffling Pig Maple
    Crackling, crushed to
    small pieces, plus extra
    to serve
streaky bacon, to serve
maple syrup, to serve

75g unsalted butter, softened, plus extra to grease
225g pitted dates
200g soft light brown sugar
225g self-raising flour
2 medium eggs, beaten
2 tablespoons golden syrup
1 teaspoon bicarbonate of soda
40g Snaffling Pig Perfectly Salted Crackling, lightly crushed

FOR THE SAUCE
75g unsalted butter
75g dark brown muscovado sugar
300ml double cream
1 tablespoon golden syrup
½ tablespoon treacle
1–2 tablespoons dark rum, optional

SALTED STICKY TOFFEE CRACKLING PUDDING

The crackling adds a welcome saltiness to this rich sweet pud, the perfect balance we think! For extra indulgence, we've added rum to our sauce, but of course this is optional.

Preheat the oven to 180°C/160°C Fan/Gas Mark 4. Grease and line the base and sides of a 20 x 25cm tin with baking parchment. In a small pan, bring the dates with 300ml of water to the boil, remove from the heat, and leave to soak for 10 minutes.

Meanwhile, in a large bowl beat together the butter, sugar, flour, eggs and golden syrup with an electric hand whisk until smooth.

Whizz the date mixture to a purée in a blender or food processor, then stir in the bicarbonate of soda. Whisk the date purée into the batter until well combined. Transfer to the prepared tin, scatter over the crackling and bake for 45–50 minutes or until a skewer inserted into the centre comes out clean.

To make the sauce, in a medium pan melt the butter, then add the sugar, double cream, golden syrup and treacle. Bring to the boil, turn down and simmer for 3–5 minutes, stirring often until thickened. Stir in the rum if using. Serve the sticky toffee pudding in slices with the sauce.

CRACKLING COOKIES

Feel free to experiment with these cookies: try adding dried cranberries, marshmallows, white chocolate or pecans; they will all work very well with the salty crackling.

Be careful not to overbake the cookies so they stay chewy; they will harden as they cool.

In a large bowl beat together the butter and sugars until the sugar has softened. Beat in the egg, then stir in the flour and baking powder. Let the mixture cool completely, before adding the chocolate and crackling. Chill the dough for 30 minutes.

Preheat the oven to 180°C/160°C Fan/Gas Mark 4. Line 3 baking sheets with baking parchment. Scoop the dough into about 15 balls and place onto the baking sheets, spaced apart (you may need to bake in batches depending on the space in your oven).

Flatten the dough balls slightly, then bake for 15–18 minutes, until just golden around the edges. Leave to cool on the baking sheets for 10 minutes, then transfer to a wire rack to cool completely.

MAKES 15

150g unsalted butter, melted and hot
150g soft light brown sugar
150g granulated sugar
1 large egg
300g plain flour
1 teaspoon baking powder
150g dark chocolate chunks
30g Snaffling Pig Maple Crackling, crushed into small pieces

LINE

THE Snaffling Pig co.

AWESOME FLAVOURED

PORK CRACKLING

LET'S MAKE THE
PIGGIN' MAGIC HAPPEN

MARVELLOUS MAPLE

EGAR

FROM THE BOTTOM OF OUR HEARTS... A PIG THANK YOU!

Luce, Aimee, Emily and all the amazing other halves of Team SP. Our super supportive families, especially Victoria (Nick's mum!) who was our first sales person.

Our brilliant chef and suppliers for buying into our idea and making the magic happen.

Then there's our awesome team, both past and present, who make every day enjoyable and really believe in rule #3 — don't be a dick.

And, we can't forget Mark from The Angel On The Bridge — our very first customer — or Rebellion Brewery for supporting us every step of the way.

Then there are legends like Eddie at Stocklake Park, Ric at Ecopac, Stu from WeLaunch, Jon Hubbard and our man Nick Ward — all of whom went above and beyond just because they're nice like that.

Sod it, we'll also thank our first accountant and a certain taller Dragon who both told us pigs would not fly, as sometimes its nice to have a little bonus drive from wanting to prove people wrong.

Finally, we really, really, really, cannot thank our customers enough; whether pubs, shops or just lovers of a porky treats, we quite literally could not do this without you.

We could probably fill a book with the people that deserve a mention here, but whilst we'd love that, it really wouldn't be the best of reads, so we'll stop here. But whether you're mentioned on here or not, if you've helped us on our journey so far we hope you know we're incredibly grateful and that we owe you all a pint.

kiss emoji

IF YOU'RE GONNA GONNA DREAM....

...YOU GOTTA DREAM PIG

First published in Great Britain by
Jon Croft Editions in 2017

info@joncrofteditions.com
www.joncrofteditions.com

This edition copyright © Snaffling Pig Co.
and Jon Croft Editions, 2017

Publisher Jon Croft
Commissioning Editor Meg Avent
Project Editor Emily North
Art Director & Senior Designer Marie O'Mara
Cover, Chapter & Slogan Page Design WeLaunch
Recipe Developer & Food Stylist Elizabeth Fox
Photography Mike Cooper
Food Styling Assistant Cassie Linford
Editor Margaret Haynes
Proofreader Zoe Ross

ISBN: 978-0-9933540-1-4

Printed in Slovenia on behalf of Latitude Press